Entrusted in Faith:

Parents, Children, and Catholic Schools

James M. Frabutt
Heidi Rocha

ALLIANCE FOR CATHOLIC EDUCATION PRESS
at the University of Notre Dame

Notre Dame, Indiana

To Molly,
wife and mother, with our thankful-
ness and love.
-Jim, Matthew, Jacob, Joshua, and Isabella

To my loving parents,
in gratitude for your support and
sacrifice throughout my 16 years of
Catholic education.
-Heidi

Copyright © 2009

Alliance for Catholic Education Press
at the University of Notre Dame
158 I.E.I. Building
Notre Dame, IN 46556
http://www.nd.edu/~acepress

ISBN: 978-0-9819501-6-7

Cover design by Mary Jo Adams Kocovski
Text design by Julie Wernick Dallavis

Title page photograph of stained glass from
Church of the Divine Child in Dearborn,
Michigan, courtesy of Mark S. Stepien.

Introduction

Imagine—or recall—the family excitement that often accompanies a child's first-ever day of kindergarten. It can be such a vibrant developmental step for the child and the young family when a son or daughter strides—hopefully with confidence, but maybe with some trepidation, too—into his or her Catholic school. The same letting go occurs in different ways and to different degrees when you attend the open house to meet your middle schooler's science teacher, or the orientation program at your Catholic high school. At these events, rife as they may be with excitement and pride, Catholic parents often engage with the more mundane aspects of the event, the particulars of everyday school life: the logistics of the school, the rules of the school handbook, the rhythm of this year's calendar, the uniform. But something deeper is missing: what about the richest truths of the faith and what the Church believes about parents and Catholic schools? Amid all else that is going on, faithful Catholic parents sometimes overlook, or have not engaged with, the deep and abiding convictions about parents and Catholic education that have emanated from popes, bishops, Canon Law, and the Magisterium.

Parents, the primary and principal educators of their children, are truly instrumental in fostering child and adolescent development, contributing immeasurably to children's social, moral, and cognitive competence.[1] Moreover, "the daily lives of parents and children contain countless instances that allow for the development of the person and therein the vitality of the whole church."[2] The family is, as the Catholic tradition has named it, a house church. Because of that undeniable developmental influence, there is a great need for parents to be well-versed in Church teaching regarding their role in Catholic schools. Drawing on over thirty Church source documents, this book outlines six major themes that form the heart of the Church's teaching regarding faith, parents, and Catholic schools.

Parents and Children's Catholic Education

Six major themes regarding parents and Catholic education emanate from key Church documents and teachings. A helpful framework for conceptualizing these themes is to consider two themes as central, foundational precepts from which the other four are derived (see schematic below). The first two themes, Primacy of Parental Role in Education and Parents as Witnesses in the World, establish what might be termed the *philosophical and theological foundations* of parents' role in Catholic education, describing the parental obligation to educate their children and importance of the parental example in faith education. The remaining four themes stem from these philosophical underpinnings, providing *practical and instrumental means* by which parents can carry out their God-given parental duties. In addition, these more applied themes enlist the aid of the entire Church community in the life of the Catholic school, demonstrating the varying levels of support offered to parents and the necessary steps toward improving Catholic education. Interested readers may consult Francis Morrisey for a helpful summary of Church teaching on parents and Catholic education as summarized in the Code of Canon Law.[3] In addition, Deborah Barton has offered a broad-based perspective on the catechetical rights, roles, and duties of Catholic parents.[4]

Primary Themes and Instrumental Subcomponents

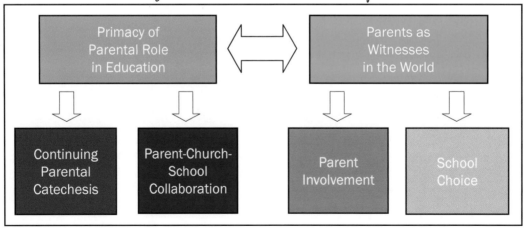

Major Themes

Primacy of Parental Role in Education	Parental duty to educate children as a fundamental responsibility of marriage, parental love as essential to the educational formation of children, care for children's learning
	Example: "Since parents have given children their life, they are bound by the most serious obligation to educate their offspring and therefore must be recognized as the primary and principal educators."[5]
Parents as Witnesses in the World	Modeling a Christian lifestyle for children, praying with children, attending weekly Mass and feast days, celebrating the Sacraments, following Church teachings, instructing children in the faith, explaining significance of Church practices and events, introducing Catholic Social Teaching, linking Christian values taught at home and in schools
	Example: "The witness of Christian life given by parents in the family comes to children with tenderness and parental respect. Children thus perceive and joyously live the closeness of God and of Jesus made manifest by their parents in such a way that this first Christian experience frequently leaves decisive traces which last throughout life."[6]
Continuing Parental Catechesis	Ensuring that parents know the fundamentals of the faith, furthering parental growth in the faith to foster Christian living in the home, linking parent and child catechesis
	Example: "A parent component must be part of many different church-sponsored educational programs. Where appropriate, Catholic schools can offer courses for parents. School-related parent organizations should provide opportunities for adults to learn more about child development and pedagogical method. Similar provision for educating and involving adults should be made by parish religious education programs."[7]
Parent-Church-School Collaboration	Partnership between parents and schools, enlisting the support of the entire Church community, pastors working with parents to secure better parent participation in and cooperation with schools, defining roles and duties of parents, establishing regional or international meetings on Catholic education
	Example: "The educational role of the Christian family therefore has a very important place in organic pastoral work. This involves a new form of cooperation between parents and Christian communities, and between the various educational groups and pastors. In this sense, the renewal of the Catholic school must give special attention both to the parents of the pupils and to the formation of a perfect educating community."[8]
Parent Involvement	Active parent participation in school activities, dialogue between parents and teachers, involvement in parent organizations aimed to improve quality of Catholic schools, alliances between parents, general support of Catholic schools
	Example: "Having chosen [a Catholic school] does not relieve [parents] of a personal duty to give their children a Christian upbringing. They are bound to cooperate actively with the school—which means supporting the educational efforts of the school and utilizing the structures offered for parental involvement, in order to make certain that the school remains faithful to Christian principles of education."[9]
School Choice	Parental right to choose Catholic schooling, expansion of parent associations endorsing school choice, support from Catholic community
	Example: "Parents who have the primary and inalienable right and duty to educate their children must enjoy true liberty in their choice of schools."[10]

Primacy of Parental Role in Education

The primary role of parents in the education of children ranks as the most central theme in regard to parents and education, cited in nearly all Church documents reviewed. This theme is especially significant given that all subsequent themes stem from parents' foremost obligation in educating their children. As one of the fundamental responsibilities of marriage, the education of children becomes inherently linked to the obligations of parenthood. Vatican II teaching on the rights of parents was forceful:

> Parents must be acknowledged as the first and foremost educators of their children. Their role as educators is so decisive that scarcely anything can compensate for their failure in it. For it devolves on parents to create a family atmosphere so animated with love and reverence for God and [persons] that a well-rounded personal and social development will be fostered among the children. Hence, the family is the first school of those social virtues which every society needs.[11]

By freely accepting God's gift of new life, parents thus hold the "grave obligation to see to the religious and moral education of their children."[12]

Parental love and care for their children serves as the foundational basis for early development and thereby contributes to childhood education, acting as a stimulus for children's motivation to learn. Parents are encouraged to readily guide the faith development of their children, thereby laying the foundation of Christianity at an early age. John Paul II elucidated this aspect of education in *Familiaris Consortio*:

> It cannot be forgotten that the most basic element, so basic that it qualifies the educational role of parents, is parental love, which finds fulfillment in the task of education as it completes and perfects its service of life: as well as being a source, the parents' love is also the animating principle and therefore the norm inspiring and guiding all concrete educational activity, enriching it with the values of kindness, constancy, goodness, service, disinterestedness and self-sacrifice that are the most precious fruit of love.[13]

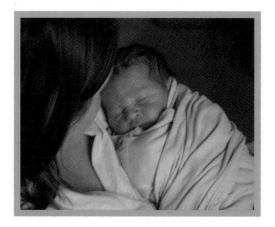

It is important to note that mothers and fathers equally share the responsibility as the primary educators in their children's lives.[14] Although in some cultures mothers have traditionally functioned as the provider of family catechesis and child development based on their natural role as childbearers, fathers also have a duty to partake in their children's learning. Both maternal and paternal collaboration in child-rearing and education enhances the standards of learning both within the home and in school.

Additionally, many documents highlighted the supreme authority of parents in directing the education of their children. Whereas teachers, administrators, and pastors in Catholic schools and parishes hold a supplementary role in nurturing child learning, the Church deems parental authority in the educational sphere as a basic right of the family. Indeed, the *Charter of the Rights of the Family* states that "since they have conferred life on their children, parents have the original,

> *By becoming parents, women and men are co-creators with God, creating and sustaining life that will itself become a source of grace and new life for others.*

primary and inalienable right to educate them; hence they must be acknowledged as the first and foremost educators of their children."[15]

Such an understanding of parenthood sees childbirth and child-rearing as a participation in the divine act of creation. By becoming parents, women and men are co-creators with God, creating and sustaining life that will itself become

a source of grace and new life for others. Inspired by the creation narrative in the very first chapters of the Bible, Catholic theology teaches that God's image resides in every person. Human dignity and worth rest on this conviction; namely, that all people are created in the divine image. One important way that this divine image reveals itself is in and through parenthood. As God has created the universe and all that is, parents participate in God's creative activity when their love, mirroring God's love, creates new life and a family.

Parents as Witnesses in the World

Complementing the primacy of parents in education is another foundational precept: Parents as Witnesses in the World. That is, about half of the examined Church documents mentioned the instructive potency of parents in witnessing their Catholic faith to their families. In *Catechesi Tradendae*, Pope John Paul II emphasized that

> education in the faith by parents, which should begin from the children's tenderest age, is already being given when the members of a family help each other to grow in faith through the witness of their Christian lives, a witness that is often without words but which perseveres throughout a day-to-day life lived in accordance with the Gospel.[16]

Given that children learn their earliest lessons in the context of family life, parents should bear in mind the power of their example and regularly

Parents further their own faith development when they instruct children in the faith through the Sacraments and religious devotions in the home.

ask themselves if their day-to-day actions reflect a Christian lifestyle. Parents should note that their example is not only witness to the moral dimensions of the faith but also to the civic and social responsibilities inherent to Catholic Social Teaching, since "the family is the first school of the social virtues."[17]

The wisdom of the Church is evident in the fact that parents further their own faith development when they instruct children in the faith through the Sacraments and religious devotions in the home. Simply attending Sunday Mass does not provide children with the faith education emphasized in the tradition of the Church. Indeed, Mass attendance might best be understood as an absolute minimum. The National Conference of Catholic Bishops indicates that "children learn to believe what their parents' words and example teach about God, and parents enrich their own faith by participating in the formal religious education of their children."[18] Through this mutual sharing, parents and children concurrently grow in Christ's love and learn to live the Gospel message more fully. The Church acknowledges the special role of parents in conveying faith by example:

> The family as a locus of catechesis has a unique privilege: transmitting the Gospel by rooting it in the context of profound human values. On this human base, Christian initiation is more profound: the awakening of the sense of God; the first steps in prayer; education of the moral conscience; formation in the Christian sense of human love, understood as a reflection of the love of God the Father, the Creator. It is, indeed, a Christian education more witnessed to than taught, more occasional than systematic, more on-going and daily than structured into periods.[19]

Additional Church documents suggest an introduction to religious education, family prayer, participation in the Sacraments (especially by regularly attending Sunday Mass), celebration of feast days, and familial acts of service for the needy as ways of fostering children's faith formation. Special care should also be given to describe the religious aspects of certain events, such as God's gift of life through birth and the joys of eternal life upon death. Thus, by following Church teaching and actively participating in Christ's message, families become more closely linked with the Church and supplement the formation conveyed in Catholic schools.

Parents themselves are in many ways sacraments to their children and to the community. If we understand a sacrament to be an outward

By following Church teaching and actively participating in Christ's message, families become more closely linked with the Church and supplement the formation conveyed in Catholic schools.

sign of an interior grace, then parents, by word and deed, can be efficacious signs to their family and to the community of God's abiding presence and power. By loving their family and serving the community, parents provide a glimpse and a reflection of God's love for us all.

Continuing Parental Catechesis

As a practical means of carrying out the duty to educate children and serve as living models of Christianity, parents must be provided with opportunities for furthering their own religious education. One third of Church texts referenced the need for advancing the faith development of parents as a means of supplementing child catechesis. Clearly, the quality of faith taught to children depends on the degree of parental understanding of the faith, which highlights the importance of this theme in Catholic education. Adequate background on the fundamentals of the Catholic faith is necessary for parents to act as witnesses to Christ's Gospel in the world.

The quality of faith taught to children depends on the degree of parental understanding of the faith.

Pastors, Catholic schools, teachers, and staff all play roles in child education; hence, Church documents underscore the need for outreach to parents that will help guide parental catechesis. For instance, Catholic school teachers should involve parents in religion projects, school Masses, or other sacramental celebrations, which would aid parent-child learning. Family events at Catholic schools and parishes such as retreats may reinvigorate the faith journey of parents and families. Explaining and engaging with the principles of Catholic Social Teaching would also be a valuable experience for both parent and child, given Christ's call to service and the need for social justice in our world. In fact, the National Conference of Catholic Bishops offered the following strategies to foster continuing parental catechesis:

> A "parent component" must be part of many different church-sponsored educational programs. Where appropriate, Catholic schools can offer courses for parents. School-related parent organizations should provide opportunities for adults to learn more about child development and pedagogical method. Similar provision for educating and involving adults should be made by parish religious education programs.[20]

Additionally, the *General Directory for Catechesis* recognizes the role of the Church community, devoting particular attention to the needs of parents: "By means of personal contact, meetings, courses and also adult catechesis directed toward parents, the Christian community must help them assume their responsibility… of educating their children in the faith."[21] By facilitating and augmenting parents' faith journeys, the Church aids parents in their marital obligation to educate their children.

Such an approach sees religious education and formation as a lifelong process, and never as something that is finished when schooling ends, or even at marriage or ordination. God's revelation continues in our lives and in our everyday experiences. As *Gaudium et Spes* remarked, the joys and hopes, the struggles and failures of the human family, are the joys and hopes, the struggles and successes of the Church. Ongoing religious formation is essential, for God is teaching us all

our lives long, calling us to new life, and inviting us to share more deeply in the dying and rising of Jesus. While Christians young and old may have a need to learn doctrine and dogma, education is only half of the equation. Mature believers need

to discern and interpret the ongoing revelation of God in their lives, and assist others to do the same. This is an important leadership responsibility for parents, as their own faith becomes a guide for their children. It is difficult, if not impossible, to be present to one's children in helpful ways regarding the presence of God in their lives if parents themselves have not been thoughtful and reflective about this same question in their own lives.

Some might say that the Catholic Church has historically been more invested in the education of the young than in the lifelong faith formation of adults. Such criticism is well-founded and highlights the need for religious formation to be understood as a developmental aspect of the faith-filled person.

Because of this manifest need, parents themselves must take steps to enhance their faith education. By praying as a family and celebrating the Sacraments, parents are reminded of their influential role in their children's lives. Moreover, "parents must not only be helped to understand the aims and methods of catechesis; they must also be involved in planning and evaluating the catechetical programs provided for their children."[22] In so doing, parents embody a spiritual thirst for learning, increase their understanding of the faith, and demonstrate their deep-seated care for mutual learning.

Parent–Church–School Collaboration

In keeping with the desire to promote a "genuine community of faith" in the Catholic school setting, over half of the reviewed Church documents noted the theme of collaboration between parents, Catholic schools, and the wider Church. Forming a strong partnership between parents, Catholic schools, and the wider Church community models an ideal Christian community, which shares in the Christian commitment to "[nourish] a life lived according to the Gospel." Such cooperation across these "principal groups that make up the educational community" will help sustain the Catholic education system and enhance the quality of Catholic schools.[23]

As the central educators in their children's lives, parents hold a special duty to join forces with teachers and administrators in Catholic schools. Merely sending one's children to Catholic school does not fulfill this "grave obligation" of education.[24] Although many extenuating factors affect working families, parents should make efforts to attend parent-teacher meetings when possible. Showing interest in their children's learning can only augment the educational experience of a child. In the same way, teachers must attempt to work with parents in the best interest of their students. The Code of Canon Law summarizes this mutual duty between parents and teachers:

> Parents must cooperate closely with the teachers of the schools to which they entrust their children to be educated; moreover, teachers in fulfilling their duty are to collaborate very closely with parents, who are to be heard willingly and for whom associations or meetings are to be established and highly esteemed.[25]

Thus, it is the official law of the Catholic Church that parents work in conjunction with teachers. Canon Law requires close cooperation and a two-way communication between parents and teachers. While most educators know that high levels of parental involvement are typically associated with academic success, the Church sees such activity as a moral and legal obligation. As much as possible, parents should collaborate with the local Church community to secure the promise of Catholic education for their children and for future students. Parents should also focus on the religious dimensions of education and work to link values learned in the school with family life.

Similarly, the Church community—both on the universal and local level—must be committed to supporting Catholic schools and parents. On a

Parents should collaborate with the local Church community to secure the promise of Catholic education for their children and for future students.

larger scale, the Church should continue to support Catholic schools, especially during difficult economic times, and take steps in the legislative and public policy arenas so that all parents have a real choice when it comes to selecting the best school for their children.

Several documents particularly noted the role of vowed religious in drawing parents into Catholic schools. In *Consecrated Persons and Their Mission in Schools,* the Sacred Congregation proclaimed:

> Consecrated persons appreciate the presence of parents in the educational community and try to establish a true relation of reciprocity with them. Participating bodies, personal meetings and other initiatives are aimed at rendering increasingly more active the insertion of parents in the life of institutions and for making them aware of the educational task.[26]

Viable suggestions for improved cooperation between these groups include hosting regular parent-school meetings, defining the roles and duties of parents in parishes and schools, launching recurrent regional or international meetings regarding Catholic education, expanding the number of safe afterschool programs, linking

the resources of the Church community with Catholic schools, and bringing pastors and parents together.[27] Additionally, advocacy for Catholic schools on behalf of the entire Church community is another essential form of collaboration for the amelioration of Catholic schools. When various "agents of education" work together to promote Catholic schooling, great strides can be made that enrich each group involved in the process.[28]

The Church has a great need for active and well-informed parent groups, and not simply for organizing fundraisers and festivals. As a way to carry out the responsibilities inherent in parenthood, parents can serve their Church, their children, and the future by becoming more politically engaged with pertinent legislative issues at the local and national level that foster equality of educational opportunity for all God's children.

Parent Involvement

Related to the previous theme of Parent-Church-School Collaboration is Parent Involvement, which focuses exclusively on parent relations with Catholic schools.

Active parent participation in school functions, increased dialogue between parents and teachers, and the establishment and bolstering of parent organizations unite parents with the mission of Catholic schools.

Nearly half of the documents note the importance of parental involvement with teachers, administration, and school activities as part of the marital duty to serve as the primary educational stakeholders in child education. Indeed, the National Conference of Catholic Bishops asserted that "neglecting parental involvement can only contribute to further misunderstanding and polarization in catechetics."[29] Moreover, the Sacred Congregation for Catholic Education describes the subsidiary duties of parents:

> Having chosen [a Catholic school] does not relieve [parents] of a personal duty to give their children a Christian upbringing. They are bound to cooperate actively with the school—which means supporting the educational efforts of the school and utilizing the structures offered for parental involvement, in order to make certain that the school remains faithful to Christian principles of education.[30]

Active parent participation in school functions, increased dialogue between parents and teachers, and the establishment and bolstering of parent organizations unite parents with the mission of Catholic schools, collaborating in order to improve the quality of education for each and every child. Although the demanding schedules of working parents can limit the hours of involvement, school activities that take place in the evenings may help draw parents into the life of the school. Parents should foster a "cordial and active relationship" with teachers to determine the best strategies to improve their child's learning and educational success.[31]

Since "parents are responsible to be involved actively in the decisions affecting the education of their children," they should join parent associations at their respective Catholic schools when possible.[32] Parents should be actively invited

to participate in school life by forging alliances with other parents in the best interests of their children. Welcoming parents into these associations will help broaden the levels of engagement, form a wider base of support, and enhance dialogue between administrators, teachers, and parents.

Parents and schools should thus work in unison for the strengthening of Catholic education.

Nonetheless, the onus of parent involvement should be considered in the context of a supportive school community. In other words, parents should not be blamed for lack of participation in their child's education, but should be welcomed into the life of the school, regardless of past participation. *The Principles for Educational Reform in the United States* states that "teachers and administrators, including boards of education, are responsible to be available to parents and collaborate with them in all decisions relating to the education of their students."[33] Parents and schools should thus work in unison for the strengthening of Catholic education.

Fundraising

TEAM SPORT COACHING

Home
And
School
Association

Parent & Teacher
Association

Volunteering

SCHOOL
BOARD

School Choice

The final theme found in nearly half of Church documents relates to the matter of school choice, which is accurately summarized in the following statement from *Gravissimum Educationis*: "Parents who have the primary and inalienable right and duty to educate their children must enjoy true liberty in their choice of schools."[34] From the earliest Church document on education, Pope Leo XIII highlighted the right of parents to choose Catholic schooling for their offspring, demonstrating the relevance of this issue from the infancy of Catholic education.[35] School choice has remained a central challenge to Catholic education up to the present era, and the Church has vigorously defended the right of parents to choose "schools that will best help them in their task as Christian educators."[36]

> *The Church has vigorously defended the right of parents to choose "schools that will best help them in their task as Christian educators."*

The Church stresses that those parents who do have the ability to send their children to Catholic school should do so in the best interest of their children's religious education and as part of their parental duty to educate. However, the financial burden of a Catholic education can be a drawback for many families who wish to send their children to Catholic schools, especially during tough economic times. Governmental aid may be a viable solution for this problem. A number of these reviewed documents alluded to the national issue of faith-based education, noting the responsibility of the State to acknowledge the right of parental school choice and to provide financial assistance to religious schools so that families have greater access to Catholic schooling. Asserting that parental rights are breached "when a compulsory system of education is imposed by the State from which all religious formation is excluded," the Pontifical Council for the Family maintained that "public authorities must ensure that public subsidies are so allocated that parents are truly free to exercise

this right without incurring unjust burdens."[37]

Moreover, school choice remains an issue not only for parents and Catholic schools, but for the entire Christian community. Provided that

School choice, properly understood, is a vehicle for establishing and protecting the equality of educational opportunity for all children.

"it is the task of the whole educative community to ensure that a distinctive Christian educational environment is maintained in practice," parent associations and Church groups should endorse school choice and serve as advocates for school choice in their local communities, thus demonstrating the Catholic community's support for Catholic education.[38]

School choice, properly understood, is a vehicle for establishing and protecting the equality of educational opportunity for all children. Many see it as a pressing social justice issue of our time. Given the reliance of public education on local property tax dollars in the U.S. and the exclusive reliance of Catholic and private schools on tuition for revenue generation, educational quality and opportunity vary widely across the nation. Per pupil costs, reflecting the dollars invested in each child's education in any given school or district, range from $6,000 to $16,000. This injustice will change only when all parents are united in demanding legislative changes, tax policies, and constitutional provisions that will establish and maintain a more equitable educational environment for all.

Vouchers

Scholarship Programs

TAX CREDITS

Financial Support for Faith-Based Schools

Documents and Themes

	Primacy of Parental Role in Education	Parents as Witnesses in the World	Continuing Parental Catechesis	Parent-Church-School Collaboration	Parent Involvement	School Choice
Spectata Fides (1885)	●					●
Sapientiae Christianae (1890)	●	●				
Divini Illius Magistri (1929)	●	●	●	●		
Mater et Magistra (1961)	●					
Lumen Gentium (1964)	●	●				
Gravissimum Educationis (1965)	●	●			●	●
Dignitatis Humanae (1965)	●					●
Gaudium et Spes (1965)	●	●				
General Directory for Catechesis (1971)	●		●	●		
To Teach as Jesus Did (1972)	●	●	●	●	●	
Evangelii Nuntiandi (1975)		●				
The Catholic School (1977)				●	●	●
Sharing the Light of Faith (1979)	●	●	●	●	●	
Catechesi Tradendae (1979)		●	●			
Familiaris Consortio (1981)	●	●			●	●
Lay Catholics in Schools (1982)	●			●		●
Code of Canon Law (1983)	●	●		●	●	●
Charter of the Rights of the Family (1983)	●	●		●	●	●
The Hispanic Presence, Challenge, and Commitment (1983)			●			

Documents and Themes

Document	Primacy of Parental Role in Education	Parents as Witnesses in the World	Continuing Parental Catechesis	Parent-Church-School Collaboration	Parent Involvement	School Choice
The Religious Dimension of Education in a Catholic School (1988)	•			•	•	
In Support of Catholic Elementary and Secondary Schools (1990)				•	•	•
Catechism of the Catholic Church (1992)	•	•	•			•
Gratissimam Sane (1994)	•	•		•	•	•
Principles for Educational Reform in the United States (1995)	•				•	•
The Catholic School on the Threshold of the Third Millennium (1997)	•			•	•	
Ecclesia in America (1999)	•	•				
Our Hearts Were Burning Within Us (1999)	•	•	•	•		
In Support of Catechetical Ministry (2000)	•			•	•	
Consecrated Persons and Their Mission in Schools (2002)	•			•	•	
Compendium of the Social Doctrine of the Church (2004)	•	•	•	•	•	•
Renewing Our Commitment to Catholic Elementary and Secondary Schools in the Third Millennium (2005)	•			•	•	•
Compendium of the Catechism of the Catholic Church (2005)	•	•				•
Educating Together in Catholic Schools (2007)	•		•	•	•	

Documents

Catholic Church. *Catechism of the Catholic Church*. London: Burns and Oates, 1999.

Congregation for Catholic Education. *The Catholic School on the Threshold of the Third Millennium*. Boston: Pauline Books and Media, 1998.

---. *Consecrated Persons and Their Mission in Schools*. London: Catholic Truth Society, 2002.

---. *Educating Together in Catholic Schools: A Shared Mission Between Consecrated Persons and the Lay Faithful*. Strathfield, NSW: St. Paul's, 2007.

Congregation for the Clergy. *General Directory for Catechesis*. Washington, DC: USCC, 1971.

Congregation for the Doctrine of the Church. *Compendium of the Catechism of the Catholic Church*. Dublin: Veritas, 2005.

John XXIII. *Mater et Magistra* [Christianity and Social Progress]. New York: Paulist, 1961.

John Paul II. *Catechesi Tradendae* [On Catechesis in Our Time]. Boston: St. Paul Editions, 1979.

---. *Familiaris Consortio* [The Role of the Christian Family in the Modern World]. Boston: Pauline Books and Media, 1981.

---. *Gratissimam Sane* [Letter to Families]. Washington, DC: USCC, 1994.

---. *Ecclesia in America*. Boston: Pauline Books and Media, 1999.

Leo XIII. *Spectata Fides* [On Christian Education]. <http://www.vatican.va/holy_father/leo_xiii/encyclicals/documents/>

---. *Sapientiae Christianae* [The Chief Duties of Christians as Citizens]. New York: Paulist, 1890.

National Conference of Catholic Bishops. *To Teach as Jesus Did: A Pastoral Message on Catholic Education*. Washington, DC: USCC, 1972.

---. *The Hispanic Presence, Challenge, and Commitment: A Pastoral Letter on Hispanic Ministry*. Washington, DC: USCC, 1983.

Paul VI. *Evangelii Nuntiandi* [On Evangelization in the Modern World]. Washington, DC: USCC, 1975.

Pius XI. *Divini Illius Magistri* [Christian Education]. Washington, DC: National Catholic Welfare Conference, 1929.

Pontifical Council for Justice and Peace. *Compendium of the Social Doctrine of the Church*. Dublin: Veritas, 2004.

Pontifical Council for the Family. *Charter of the Rights of the Family*. Washington, DC: USCC, 1983.

Pontifical Council for the Revision of the Code of Canon Law. *Codes Juris Canonici* [Code of Canon Law]. Washington, DC: Canon Law Society of America, 1983.

Sacred Congregation for Catholic Education. *The Catholic School*. Washington, DC: USCC, 1977.

---. *Lay Catholics in Schools: Witnesses to Faith*. Boston: St. Paul Editions, 1982.

---. *The Religious Dimension of Education in a Catholic School*. Washington, DC: USCC, 1988.

United States Catholic Conference. *Sharing the Light of Faith: National Catechetical Directory for Catholics in the United States*. Washington, DC: USCC, 1979.

---. *Principles of Educational Reform in the United States*. Washington, DC: USCC, 1995.

---. *In Support of Catechetical Ministry: A Statement of the U.S. Catholic Bishops*. Washington, DC: USCC, 2000.

United States Conference of Catholic Bishops. *In Support of Catholic Elementary and Secondary Schools*. Washington, DC: USCCB, 1990.

---. *Our Hearts Were Burning Within Us: A Pastoral Plan for Adult Faith Formation in the United States*. Washington, DC: USCCB, 1999.

---. *Renewing Our Commitment to Catholic Elementary and Secondary Schools in the Third Millennium*. Washington, DC: USCCB, 2005.

Vatican Council II. *Lumen Gentium* [On the Church]. New York: Holt, Rinehart, and Winston, 1964.

---. *Dignitatis Humanae* [Declaration on Religious Freedom]. New York: Paulist, 1965.

---. *Gaudium et Spes* [On the Church in the Modern World]. Washington, DC: National Catholic Welfare Conferemce, 1965.

---. *Gravissimum Educationis* [On Christian Education]. Washington, DC: National Catholic Welfare Conference, 1965.

Conclusion

Parenting brings with it tremendous joys and awesome responsibilities. This book has highlighted the exalted role parents occupy in the teaching of the Catholic Church, and the essential role they play in the ongoing education of their children and the sanctification of the entire human family. The authors hope that this analysis, richly laden with citations from official Church documents, will serve as an inspiration and support for parents in the important role God has called them to fulfill.

Notes

[1] J. M. Frabutt, "Parenting in Contemporary Society: Exploring the Links with Children's Social, Moral, and Cognitive Competence," in *Handbook of Research on Catholic Education*, eds. T. C. Hunt, E. A. Joseph, and R. J. Nuzzi (Westport, CT: Greenwood Press, 2001), 181-204.

[2] J. M. Frabutt, "Parents: The Primary and Principal Educators," in *Catholic Schools Still Make a Difference: Ten Years of Research*, eds. T. C. Hunt, E. A. Joseph, and R. J. Nuzzi (Washington, DC: National Catholic Educational Association, 2002), 73.

[3] F. G. Morrisey, "The Rights of Parents in the Education of Their Children (Canons 796-806)," *Studia Canonica 23* (1989): 429-444.

[4] D. A. Barton, "Education and Catechesis of Children: Rights of Parents and Rights of Bishops," *Canon Law Society of America Proceedings 62* (2000): 63-92.

[5] Vatican Council II, *Gravissimum Educationis* (Washington, DC: National Catholic Welfare Conference, 1965), par. 3.

[6] Congregation for the Clergy, *General Directory for Catechesis* (Washington, DC: United States Catholic Conference, 1971), par. 226.

[7] National Conference of Catholic Bishops, *To Teach as Jesus Did: A Pastoral Message on Catholic Education* (Washington, DC: United States Catholic Conference, 1972), par. 59.

[8] John Paul II, *Familiaris Consortio* (Boston: Pauline Books and Media, 1981), par. 40.

[9] Sacred Congregation for Catholic Education, *The Catholic School* (Washington, DC: United States Catholic Conference, 1977), par. 73.

[10] Vatican Council II, *Gravissimum Educationis*, par. 6.

[11] Ibid., par. 3.

[12] Pontifical Commission for the Revision of the Code of Canon Law, *Code of Canon Law* (Washington, DC: Canon Law Society of America, 1983), Canon 1113.

[13] John Paul II, *Familiaris Consortio*, par. 36.

[14] Vatican Council II, *Gravissimum Educationis*, par. 3.

[15] Pontifical Council for the Family, *Charter of the Rights of the Family* (Washington, DC: United States Catholic Conference, 1983), §5.

[16] John Paul II, *Catechesi Tradendae* (Boston: St. Paul Editions, 1979), par. 68.

[17] Vatican Council II, *Gravissimum Educationis*, par. 3.

[18] National Conference of Catholic Bishops, *To Teach as Jesus Did*, par. 25.

[19] Congregation for the Clergy, *General Directory for Catechesis*, par. 255.

[20] National Conference of Catholic Bishops, *To Teach as Jesus Did*, par. 59.

[21] Congregation for the Clergy, *General Directory for Catechesis*, par. 227.

[22] National Conference of Catholic Bishops, *To Teach as Jesus Did*, par. 55.

[23] Sacred Congregation for Catholic Education, *Lay Catholics in Schools: Witnesses to Faith* (Boston: St. Paul Editions, 1982), par. 41.

[24] Pius XI, *Divini Illius Magistri* (Washington, DC: National Catholic Welfare Conference, 1929), par. 34.

[25] Pontifical Commission for the Revision of the Code of Canon Law, *Code of Canon Law*, Canon 796, §2.

[26] Congregation for Catholic Education, *Consecrated Persons and Their Mission in Schools* (London: Catholic Truth Society, 2002), par. 47.

[27] Congregation for Catholic Education, *Educating Together in Catholic Schools: A Shared Mission Between Consecrated Persons and the Lay Faithful* (Strathfield, NSW: St. Paul's, 2007), par. 48-49, 51.

[28] John Paul II, *Familiaris Consortio*, par. 40.

[29] National Conference of Catholic Bishops, *To Teach as Jesus Did*, par. 56.

[30] Sacred Congregation for Catholic Education, *The Catholic School*, par. 73.

[31] John Paul II, *Familiaris Consortio*, par. 40.

[32] United States Catholic Conference, *Principles for Educational Reform in the United States* (Washington, DC: Author, 1995), §B-2.

[33] Ibid., §B-4.

[34] Vatican Council II, *Gravissimum Educationis*, par. 6.

[35] Leo XIII, *Sapientiae Christianae* (New York: Paulist Press, 1890), par. 42.

[36] Catholic Church, *Catechism of the Catholic Church* (London: Burns and Oates, 1999), §2229.

[37] Pontifical Council for the Family, *Charter of the Rights of the Family*, §5.

[38] Sacred Congregation for Catholic Education, *The Catholic School*, par. 73.

About the Authors

James M. Frabutt is Faculty in The Mary Ann Remick Leadership Program in the Alliance for Catholic Education and Concurrent Associate Professor of Psychology at the University of Notre Dame. With colleagues in the Remick Leadership Program, he has co-authored two books, *Research, Action, and Change: Leaders Reshaping Catholic Schools*, and *Faith, Finances, and the Future: The Notre Dame Study of U.S. Pastors*. He has employed action-oriented, community-based research approaches to areas such as juvenile delinquency prevention, school-based mental health, teacher/administrator inquiry, racial disparities in the juvenile justice system, and community violence reduction. He holds a B.A. in Psychology and Italian from the University of Notre Dame and a Master's degree and Ph.D. in Human Development and Family Studies from the University of North Carolina at Greensboro.

Heidi Rocha teaches second grade at Cathedral Academy in New Orleans, Louisiana, as part of the Alliance for Catholic Education Service Through Teaching program. She has conducted case studies of the quality of education for ESL students in Park City, Utah, and has researched the levels of social and civic responsibility for middle school students in South Bend, Indiana. She holds a B.A. in American Studies with minors in Catholic Social Tradition and Education, Schooling, and Society from the University of Notre Dame.

LaVergne, TN USA
29 September 2009
159372LV00002B